"Go and make disciples of all nations, baptizing them in the name of the Father and of the Son and of the Holy Spirit, and teaching them to obey all that I have commanded you" (Matt. 28:19–20).

The Great Commission encompasses the whole task of the church. And here is help for fulfilling that task—the DISCIPLING RESOURCES series. Designed for small-group use, whether Bible study, Sunday school, or fellowship groups, this effective approach is firmly based on biblical principles of disciple building.

Each group member receives his or her own copy of the book, which guides the group through thirteen weekly meetings. Every step of the group- and personal-study process is included, plus biblical material and commentary. Leaders need only facilitate participation. This series is designed to increase knowledge of God's Word, cultivate supportive personal relationships, and stimulate spiritual growth—an adventure in being His disciples.

Titles in this exciting new series:

Available now

Basic Christian Values
First Steps for New and Used Christians
Fruit of the Spirit
The Good Life (Rom. 12–16)

Projected

Being Christ's Church (Ephesians)
Discipling Your Emotions
Developing Personal Responsibility
A Life of Fellowship (1 John)

FIRST STEPS
FOR
NEW & USED CHRISTIANS

LARRY RICHARDS
NORM WAKEFIELD

ZONDERVAN BIBLE PUBLISHERS
OF THE ZONDERVAN CORPORATION
1415 LAKE DRIVE, S.E. | GRAND RAPIDS, MI 49506

FIRST STEPS FOR NEW AND USED CHRISTIANS
© 1981 by The Zondervan Corporation

Second printing 1982

Portions of this material first appeared in Larry Richard's *Born to Grow* (Wheaton, Ill.: Victor Books, a division of SP publications, 1974), and are used by permission.

Library of Congress Cataloging in Publication Data

Richards, Lawrence O
    First steps for new and used Christians.

    (Discipling resources)
    "Correlated with Born to grow, by Larry Richards."
    1. Christian life—Study and teaching. I. Wakefield, Norm, joint author. II. Richards, Lawrence O. Born to grow. III. Title. IV. Series.
BV3411.R52   248.4   80-29188
ISBN 0-310-43411-4

Unless indicated otherwise, Scripture references are from the Holy Bible: New International Version, copyright © 1978 by the New York International Bible Society.

Edited by Mary Bombara
Designed by Mary Bombara and Martha Bentley

CONTENTS

WELCOME HOME

You've been on a
long and lonely journey.
It hasn't been easy.
And all along
you've missed the sense
of belonging:
of really being *loved*.
Well, good news!
In Christ
you've come *home!*

DRAW
a picture here
of the place
you have felt most
"at home."

What feelings
do you associate
with this place
you've drawn?

_____

_____

_____

_____

_____

_____

_____

_____

_____

_____

Together, each describe the feelings and tell what about the
place you drew made it "home" to you. Take all the time
you need.

A Word from Larry

Christianity is a relationship. This may be a familiar phrase, but let's think for a moment about what it means.

You are not a Christian because of what you do or do not do. You are a child of God through your personal trust in Jesus Christ as your Savior.

Trust in Jesus was, using a biblical picture, a "new birth" for you. You were born into a family, in which God Himself is your Father. You are a child of God. He Himself affirms that *you belong!*

What's more, the family into which you were born is a large one. You have a host of brothers and sisters. And each of these brothers and sisters has the capacity to love you. And in the family, you discover that you too have the capacity to love them! If you have ever felt isolated and alone and longed for intimacy, you'll see how important that gift of love within the family can be.

As you grow as a Christian you will learn many things that you will believe. As you grow you will find many of your actions and attitudes changing. But as you grow you will find nothing is more important to you—and to God—than to expand your capacity to accept and enjoy His great gift of love; to expand your own experience of loving God and being loved by Him; and to expand your experience of loving others, and being loved by them.

WHICH
of these
passages best
communicates to
you that as a
Christian you
truly are "at
home" with God?

This is how God showed his love among us: he sent his one and only Son into the world that we might live through him.
1 John 4:9

How great is the love the Father has lavished on us, that we should be called the children of God! And that is what we are!
1 John 3:1

For I am convinced that neither death nor life, neither angels nor demons, neither the present nor the future, nor any powers, neither height nor depth, nor anything else in all creation, will be able to separate us from the love of God that is in Christ Jesus our Lord.
Romans 8:38-39

But because of his great love for us, God, who is rich in mercy, made us alive with Christ even when we were dead in trespasses—it is by grace you have been saved.
Ephesians 2:4–5

Therefore, since we have been justified through faith, we have peace with God through our Lord Jesus Christ.
Romans 5:1

Both the one who makes men holy and those who are made holy are of the same family. So Jesus is not ashamed to call them brothers.
Hebrews 2:11

SHARE
with the others
what it is
about the verse
you chose
that is most
meaningful
to you.

Partners

Discipleship is more than "learning." It means growing and putting what each one learns into daily practice. To encourage this and to help you each experience a growing love (belonging) relationship, this course invites you to take part in two disciplines.

First, each study includes a daily journal. Jot down your meditation notes and what God is teaching you from Scripture. Also record what happens in your daily experience as you live this adventure with Him.

Second, you will be teamed with another person, to live through this First Steps adventure together. Your responsibility will be to (1) pray for your partner daily, and (2) meet with your partner or talk with him or her by phone at least once during the week. You may want to get together for coffee or for lunch. But when you are together, share what you have recorded in your journal.

Here is space to jot down your partner's name, address, and phone number and your weekly appointment time. Do take time *now* to pair off in partnership teams.

My partner's name _____

My partner's address _____

_____

My partner's phone _____

Appointment time _____

Appointment place _____

THIS WEEK

Select one of the verses from page 11 to *memorize*. Choose one which you would like as your personal "theme" verse for this 13-week adventure.

JOURNAL

What is God teaching you through His Word? Through daily experiences? Jot down your meditations.

DAY 1

DAY 2

DAY 3

DAY 4

DAY 5

DAY 6

YOU'RE LOVED

Sometimes
even good parents
love conditionally—
we have to "fit in"
for them to accept us.
In God's family
we're loved
just as we are.
Forever.

Billy's done it
again!

Write here what each is saying or thinking about Billy.

DAD   BROTHER OR SISTER   BILLY

_____   _____   _____

_____   _____   _____

_____   _____   _____

_____   _____   _____

_____   _____   _____

_____   _____   _____

Discuss

1 Share your impressions of people's reactions to Billy.

2 When you were a child, did people ever react to you this way? Tell about one experience.

3 Are there ever times when it seems to you God must feel this way about you as a Christian?

READ
this Scripture
passage.

Romans 8
tells of
God's loving choice
of you and me
to be *His*.

It also asks
if He now
condemns
or loves us.

Underline
the one verse
or phrase
that convinces *you*
that you are loved . . .
no matter what!

What, then, shall we say in response to this? If God is for us, who can be against us? He who did not spare his own Son, but gave him up for us all—how will he not also, along with him, graciously give us all things? Who will bring any charge against those whom God has chosen? It is God who justifies. Who is he that condemns? Christ Jesus, who died—more than that, who was raised to life—is at the right hand of God and is also interceding for us. Who shall separate us from the love of Christ? Shall trouble or hardship or persecution or famine or nakedness or danger or sword? As it is written:

> "For your sake we face death all day long;
> we are considered as sheep to be slaughtered."

No, in all these things we are more than conquerors through him who loved us. For I am convinced that neither death nor life, neither angels nor demons, neither the present nor the future, nor any powers, neither height nor depth, nor anything else in all creation, will be able to separate us from the love of God that is in Christ Jesus our Lord.

Romans 8:31-39

God is a unique Person.
He is *pure love* . . .
along with
goodness, holiness, and justice.

How does pure love
view those who are children
in His family?

We have to be careful always
not to judge
how God might feel or act
on the basis of how
others who have
cared for us
have reacted to us.
Human love,
even when real,
is not always pure love,
or even wise love.

Let's think more
about this Romans passage
and see what God means
when He says to us,
"I love you."
And see more
of the kind of Person
He is.

TOGETHER

Read
each verse
and the
commentary
below it. Compare
and contrast
what it reveals about
God's love
with the love
you have received
from other people.

Share your insights
with the whole group.

As others
give illustrations,
write them in.

VERSE

He who did not spare his own Son, but gave him up for us all—how will he not also, along with him, graciously give us all things?

COMMENTARY

How special are we? The specialness God demonstrated in creation fades to insignificance when we see our importance affirmed in Christ's death. God didn't spare His own Son. God gave Jesus, and Jesus offered Himself, to die for us. *You were so important to God that He gave His dearest and His best to bring you into His family.*

So never feel about yourself as Jan did about herself. Never feel you are worthless, that you don't count. God set His own price tag on you. And that price tag reads "Jesus."

You are worth His life—and death.*

COMPARISON/CONTRAST ILLUSTRATIONS

_____

_____

_____

_____

_____

_____

*Larry Richards, *Born to Grow* (Wheaton, Ill.: Victor Books, 1974), p. 20.

VERSE

What, then, shall we say in response to this? If God is for us, who can be against us?

COMMENTARY

How do we react when we realize that we really are special? Paul, the author of the letter, states it as a question: "If God is for us, who can be against us?"

Jan's parents took a stand against her as a person. They tried to make her feel unimportant, worthless. But should Jan continue to let her father's view shape her feelings about herself? Or should Jan—and you and I—realize that all the negative, criticizing people who make us cringe and reject our specialness are *wrong?* The great and amazing fact is that *God* is *for* us. He stands against the critics and affirms, *"You are special. You are important to Me."**

COMPARISON/CONTRAST ILLUSTRATIONS

_____

_____

_____

_____

_____

_____

*Ibid.

VERSE

Who will bring any charge against those whom God has chosen? It is God who justifies. Who is he that condemns? Christ Jesus, who died—more than that, who was raised to life—is at the right hand of God and is also interceding for us.

COMMENTARY

It's hard to feel important and valuable when we fall short of what we want to be or feel we ought to be. Yet we all do fall short. We let ourselves be pulled away from God, we dabble in sin, we feel our love for Jesus grow cold. And then we accuse ourselves and say, "See! I *knew* I was worthless. I knew I wasn't special. Because if I were special, I couldn't behave this way.

These verses in Romans warn us not to bring charges like these against ourselves. As a Christian we will fail . . . often. And when we do, we'll feel guilty and bad about ourselves. But God has taken care of that sin in Jesus' death. He has "justified" us—and that means he has both forgiven us of sin and declared us to be upright in His eyes. He doesn't see us as worthless sinners; Jesus continually intercedes for us.

God sees you as a child whom He loves.

In Christ we learn to look at ourselves from an entirely new perspective. Our specialness, our worth, our being loved, do not depend on what we do. We're special, worthy, loved, because of *who we are.* And who are we? Who are you? You are a person whom God loves and who He declares is special to Him!*

COMPARISON/CONTRAST ILLUSTRATIONS

_____

_____

_____

_____

*Ibid., pp. 20–21.

Thank God for His kind of love.

If there is time
left, complete page 24
before having your
prayer time.

WRITE

Meditate
on God's
kind of
love.

Then
write a
prayer
thanking
Him for
loving
you as
He does.

_____

_____

_____

_____

_____

_____

_____

_____

_____

_____

_____

_____

_____

THIS WEEK

1 Pray your prayer daily when you talk with God.

2 Read your prayer to your partner when you meet.

3 Memorize the following verse this week.

The Lord is gracious and compassionate,
  slow to anger and rich in love.
The Lord is good to all;
  he has compassion on all he has made.

Psalm 145:8–9

JOURNAL

DAY 1

DAY 2

DAY 3

DAY 4

DAY 5

DAY 6

27

YOU'RE FORGIVEN **3**

Many people suffer
with guilt feelings.
They try
to get rid of them
in many ways—
by payment,
by denial,
by pretending.
But God
has a better way
to deal
with your guilt.

DEFINITIONS

Real Guilt	**Guilt Feelings**
specific wrong acts of sin	subjective reactions to real or imagined wrong actions
involves personal responsibility for own actions	may or may not be related to responsible actions— others' reactions may make me "feel guilty"
deserves punishment by God	involve self-punishment

My *feelings* may or may not be related to acts of sin. And my feelings are not the basic issue with God. God helps me straighten out my feelings by dealing with *real guilt.*

God did not give us a sense of guilt to torment us, but to alert us to the reality of sin.

This is a basic thing to get in mind about guilt. It should always direct our attention to Jesus!

Forgiveness is the Bible's teaching on how God deals with real guilt to free me for a happy, confident, and holy life with Him.

How God deals with Guilt

STUDY

the material
on these pages carefully.
When you believe
you have mastered
the key concepts,
close the book
and try
to explain them to
your partner.
Work together
as partners until
you are sure
you both understand
what the Bible says
about guilt
and forgiveness.

In the New Testament, "guilt" is mentioned only six times—and only sixteen times in the Old. But sixty times in the New Testament alone God speaks of forgiveness. In most of these cases, forgiveness is directly related to sin, which is the root of guilt. God doesn't only deal with guilt, the result. In Christ He has dealt decisively with sin, the cause!

The words translated "forgive" are fascinating to explore. In the Old Testament, the major word means, literally, *to send off.* Psalm 103:2-3 KJV blesses the Lord as One who *pardons* (literally, *sends off*) all our iniquities. And through Jeremiah God promises in the coming Christ, "I will forgive *(send off)* their iniquity, and I will remember their sin no more" (Jer. 31:34, KJV).

The New Testament picks up the same theme, with one word that emphasizes *be gracious to* and another that restates the Old Testament term: *send off.* So God says, "Be kind to one another, tenderhearted, forgiving each other, just as God in Christ also has forgiven you" (Eph. 4:32). Instead of responding to sin with the judgment it deserves, God has determined to be gracious. He reaches out in love to touch the sinner. Touching us in love, He *sends off* our sin.

This is why we come to Jesus when we sense guilt. Jesus continues to *send off* sin. He knows our inadequacies and how prone to failure we are. He touches us, and sends away our weaknesses. Jesus knows our perverseness and how quick we are to turn to our own way. He touches us, and sends away the results of our willfulness and the willfulness itself. *And then He remembers our sins no more.* *

*Richards, *Born to Grow,* p. 33.

31

DRAW

God wants us to realize that as forgiven persons our sins themselves truly have been "sent away."

Here are some passages that contain word pictures designed to help us realize that because of Jesus our sins truly are gone.

Select *one* that is meaningful to you, look it up, and draw a picture of what God has done with *your* sins.

Psalm 103:12
Micah 7:19
Isaiah 38:17
Isaiah 1:18

INDIVIDUALLY

Recall a time
when you were aware
that you had sinned.
Put a check mark
beside each
of the following activities
that you
would have felt comfortable
undertaking then.

_____ Witnessing to your neighbor about Jesus
_____ Making a request to God in prayer
_____ Reading your Bible
_____ Sharing something personal about yourself with another Christian
_____ Encouraging someone else who is discouraged
_____ Welcoming a visit from your pastor
_____ Playing with your children
_____ Starting a new project at work or home
_____ Taking on a ministry with other Christians
_____ Singing in church worship service
_____ Going to church
_____ Telling your spouse you love him or her
_____ Telling God you love Him

Recall a time when you were especially aware of forgiveness for a specific sin. Go back over the list and put a cross beside each of the activities you would have felt comfortable undertaking then.

Before turning the page, share the results with each other.

WRITE DOWN
one word that summarizes the effect of forgiveness on a person's life.

_____

DISCUSS
the word
each person chose,
and why.

A Word from Norm

Read
and discuss
in class
if time allows.

God has outlined a simple, clear process that leads to forgiveness. He has designed a process which liberates His children from defeat and despair. We have no need to dwell in the pits of guilty feelings . . . or, to rationalize our failures because we fear to face them.

First John 1:8-9 describes the steps leading to forgiveness. We begin with *honesty.* Verse 8 suggests that we can deceive ourselves by denying sin in our lives. When we have specifically disobeyed God we need to be honest with ourselves and admit it. "I have sinned in gossiping about Mr. Edwards."

Once we have been honest with ourselves, we can be honest with God. This leads to the second step of *confession.* "Father, I admit that I have sinned. I have gossiped about Mr. Edwards. I ask Your forgiveness." Since God is gracious . . . eager to forgive, I have no need to hide, excuse, or rationalize my sin.

Now we are ready to take the third step of *thankful trust.* We thank God that He *has* forgiven us, and trust what He has said, rather than what we may feel. "If we confess our sins, he *is* faithful and just and *will* forgive us our sins and purify us from all unrighteousness" (v. 9). We must base our forgiveness on what God says He will do, not on our feelings.

When we take these steps they lead us to experience God's gracious forgiveness. His boundless love has provided a way whereby we, His children, can live in peace and joy.

THIS WEEK

Privately,
if any
of these experiences
happen to you,
come back
to this page
and write down
God's verdict
after your confession:
"I'm forgiven."

Have you been disappointed in yourself and ashamed of your failure to follow Jesus as fully as you wish?

_____

Have you made choices that you knew were wrong and come to feel that you've lost all right to hope for God's mercy?

_____

Have you pushed yourself to do the "right thing" because you felt you ought to, or to avoid the anguish of guilt?

_____

Have you built walls of self-righteousness to protect you from the failures you're too ashamed to face and to admit?

_____

Have you been bitter and critical of others, disappointed in them and angry at them at the same time? *

_____

*The above material is from Richards, _Born to Grow,_ p. 39.

So live as a forgiven person.

Journal

MEMORIZE 1 JOHN 1:9

DAY 1

DAY 2

DAY 3

DAY 4

DAY 5

DAY 6

YOU'RE ACCEPTED

Not perfect yet?
And troubled
about your imperfections?
Most of us are
at one time or another.
At times like these
we each need
to understand
what God means
when He says,
"You're accepted."

READ

Here is a paragraph
Larry wrote about
his two sons.

I have a ten-year-old son, Tim, who looks up to his teen-age brother, Paul, and tries to do the same things Paul does. Usually he can; Tim's a well-developed child. But every now and then there's something he can't do as well, and it frustrates him terribly. He sees Paul driving for the basket and making a reverse lay-up. When he tries, too often the ball won't go in. So Tim gets frustrated and upset. Paul shoots his air pistol with great accuracy. Tim's getting good, but he's not good enough. Paul, who plans to be an artist, can draw and paint with great skill. Tim is good for a 10-year-old, but his pictures don't look like Paul's.*

DISCUSS

1 Why does Tim have difficulty in accepting himself?

2 How do you think Paul feels about Tim?

3 How do you think I feel about Tim as his dad?

4 Are Tim's feelings of frustration understandable? Are they valid?

*Richards, *Born to Grow*, p. 43.

QUIZ

Sometimes Christians are frustrated with themselves also. Take this quiz on your frustration level (check appropriate space).

	SELDOM	SOMETIMES	USUALLY
1 I feel discouraged because I'm not growing fast enough.	_____	_____	_____
2 I feel angry at my lack of self-discipline.	_____	_____	_____
3 I'm ashamed that some of my old habits have not disappeared.	_____	_____	_____
4 I'm afraid that I do not really please God.	_____	_____	_____
5 I would be ashamed to have other people know my doubts and thoughts.	_____	_____	_____
6 I feel guilty because I don't talk to others about Christ.	_____	_____	_____
7 I feel useless when I compare myself to other Christians.	_____	_____	_____
8 I feel trapped because of my past failures.	_____	_____	_____

READ
Now, here is Larry's reaction
to his son Tim's problem.

It's so hard for Tim to realize that age and experience account for these skills of Paul's. And that he can't expect to do everything as well as a teen-ager.

Age plays a part in the Christian's life too. It's through time that we mature as we gain more experience of God's ways. As Hebrews 5:14 says, the "adult" believer is the one who "has developed by experience his power to discriminate between what is good and what is evil" (PHILLIPS).

I try to help Tim accept himself *as he is.* But it's hard when he so badly wants the results of the growth process—without having to take the time to grow!

In a way, all of life testifies to us that we are to accept ourselves as incomplete and to be glad for our present stage of development.*

What principles here do you think God wants us to apply in understanding and accepting ourselves?

Decide together.

_____

_____

_____

_____

_____

*Ibid., pp. 43–44.

**God wants us
to accept ourselves
as incomplete
persons.**

God wants us to grow gradually toward perfection.

READ

this Scripture
passage.

WHAT IS THE KEY TO GROWTH? In groups of six talk about what each underlined phrase tells you about your personal spiritual growth.

I am the true vine and my Father is the gardener. He cuts off every branch in me that bears no fruit, while <u>every branch that does bear fruit he trims clean so that it will be even more fruitful.</u> You are already clean because of the word I have spoken to you. <u>Remain in me, and I will remain in you.</u> No branch can bear fruit by itself; it must remain in the vine. Neither can you bear fruit unless you remain in me.

I am the vine; you are the branches. <u>If a man remains in me and I in him, he will bear much fruit;</u> apart from me you can do nothing. If anyone does not remain in me, he is like a branch that is thrown away and withers; such branches are picked up, thrown into the fire and burned. If you remain in me and my words remain in you, ask whatever you wish, and it will be given you. This is to my Father's glory, that you bear much fruit, showing yourselves to be my disciples.

As the Father has loved me, so have I loved you. Now <u>remain in my love. If you obey my commands, you will remain in my love,</u> just as I have obeyed my Father's commands and remain in his love. <u>I have told you this so that my joy may be in you and that your joy may be complete.</u>

John 15:1-11

A Word from Larry

Here is a summary of the key truths explored this session. In the space provided, *initial* each paragraph with which you agree.

It is often hard for us to accept ourselves as Christians and to realize that God actually accepts us, right where we are now. All too often our idea of acceptability focuses on what we cannot do, not on what we can do and are doing. Like a child who wants desperately to be grown up, we want to be grown up spiritually—right now. And when something that reveals us to be children still occurs we are disappointed and frustrated and find it very hard to accept ourselves or to believe that God could be pleased with us. _____

But our Christian life is a life that matures through a growth process. We do not mature overnight. And it does take time for us to grow. Like any Father, God is pleased at our progress and does not demand that we be perfect before our time. _____

While we can then accept ourselves as imperfect persons and know that God accepts us as imperfect too, we do want to keep on growing. The focus in our life should not be on how far we have come, but on "are we growing?" And John 15 helps us see how to grow. How do we grow? First, by building our personal relationship with Jesus, and staying close to Him. Second, by realizing that we are dependent on him for everything, and acting by faith in him rather than trust in ourselves. Third, by glorifying God for the changes he makes in us as we grow. And finally, by letting *joy in the process* replace guilt and shame and frustration at the fact we still have further to grow than we've come. _____

Because God has accepted me, I can accept myself, and I am free now to *grow.* _____

QUIZ

As these truths become more and more a part of your outlook and your life, your feelings about yourself will change.

Take this quiz now, imagining that you have lived all of this coming week by the truths you initialed on the preceeding page.

	SELDOM	SOMETIMES	USUALLY
1 I feel discouraged because I'm not growing fast enough.	_____	_____	_____
2 I feel angry at my lack of self-discipline.	_____	_____	_____
3 I'm ashamed that some of my old habits have not disappeared.	_____	_____	_____
4 I'm afraid that I do not really please God.	_____	_____	_____
5 I would be ashamed to have other people know my doubts and thoughts.	_____	_____	_____
6 I feel guilty because I don't talk to others about Christ.	_____	_____	_____
7 I feel useless when I compare myself to other Christians.	_____	_____	_____
8 I feel trapped because of my past failures.	_____	_____	_____

THIS WEEK

Meditate on each "growth" statement before you write in your journal each day. Memorize John 15:8.

JOURNAL

DAY 1   Growth is my relationship with Jesus.

DAY 2   Growth is my response to what God is teaching me.

DAY 3   Growth is God's power giving me new strength.

Growth is Christ's wisdom giving me new perspectives on life. **DAY 4**

Growth is Christ's love enabling me to work through problems. **DAY 5**

Growth is Christ's presence, giving me strength to cope. **DAY 6**

YOU'RE NOT ALONE $\boxed{5}$

That may sound like
a promise.
To some people
it's a threat.
What does it mean
for a Christian
to be part of
a community
in which he needs
others . . . and others need
him?

CHECK (√)

Which
of these
have been
true of
your experience
in the past?

_____ 1 I just can't trust others. They always let me down.

_____ 2 I've been rejected so much in the past I'd rather not get close to people.

_____ 3 People are so shallow that I just prefer to get off by myself.

_____ 4 My work keeps me too busy to spend time with people.

_____ 5 I've found people are only friendly as long as they can get something out of me.

_____ 6 I try not to be too personal because I think a person's private life should be private.

_____ 7 I've noticed that no one is really interested in what any other person is going through, anyway.

_____ 8 I'm only comfortable with people who are like me.

_____ 9 I've always been able to do a good job at being superficially friendly.

_____ 10 I can't remember truly caring for another person deeply.

_____ 11 Since I've never been close to people, the thought of closeness is frightening.

SELECT

one of the statements
you checked (if any)
which is most significant
to you.

SHARE

it with
the rest
of your group.
Also, share
any experiences
which the statement
brought to mind.

THEN

You
have been talking
about your *past*
experience.

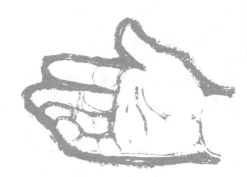

NOW

Think about
this new
experience:

"You are the body of Christ, and each one of you is a part of it."

1 Corinthians 12:27

READ

What will it
mean to you
to be part
of the Body
of Christ?
Think about
the analogy
of a "body"
in this
passage.

The eye cannot say to the hand, "I don't need you!" And the head cannot say to the feet, "I don't need you!" On the contrary, those parts of the body that seem to be weaker are indispensable, and the parts that we think are less honorable we treat with special honor. And the parts that are unpresentable are treated with special modesty, while our presentable parts need no special treatment. But God has combined the members of the body and has given greater honor to the parts that lacked it, so that there should be no division in the body, but that its parts should have equal concern for each other. If one part suffers, every part suffers with it; if one part is honored, every part rejoices with it.

1 Corinthians 12:21-26

LIST

Work with your partner
to list statements
about the kinds of relationships
you will have with other Christians.

_____

_____

_____

_____

_____

_____

_____

_____

_____

SHARE
your insights
with your whole group.

THINK BACK

over your experiences
in this discipling group
and your experiences with your partner.

Which of the kinds
of relationships
you listed (p. 57)
have you experienced?

SHARE

Take time *now,* with the whole
group, to tell of that experience
and thank anyone who made
a special contribution to it.

A Word from Norm

Growth as a Christian involves growing in our ability to relate to each other as members of Christ's Body.

Each of the deepening qualities of the relationships you discovered in 1 Corinthians 12 will more and more be yours as one of Christ's most wonderful gifts to us.

These relationships are potentially yours now—no matter what your past experience is like. But we each need to grow into their full experience. This growing does involve taking initiative—reaching out to people who are hesitant, waiting for someone else to take the lead. And really, beginning to build Christian relationships with others is not difficult.

Here are just a few settings in which you might take initiative to grow in your relationship with others. Look them over and see which seem most natural and easy for you.

Some of these are better for building relationships than others, and some you'll feel more comfortable with. Select which of the settings listed you feel most comfortable with and record your preference in the spaces provided.

make a phone call
have lunch together
meet to pray together
invite home for a meal
send a note in the mail
attend church regularly
get together to help a friend
visit a hospital
join a church committee
take vacation trip together by families
have people in to stay overnight
share family work projects (like lawn work)
write a book together
go fishing
take in social event together (movie, bowling)
take out a neighbor's kids

Most effective and comfortable for me.

_____

_____

_____

Least effective and comfortable for me.

_____

_____

_____

THIS WEEK

Look over the list in "A Word from Norm." Choose one idea that you would like to act on this week to build a closer relationship with another person.

Journal

MEMORIZE JOHN 13:34–35.

___

DAY 1

___

DAY 2

___

DAY 3

DAY 4

DAY 5

DAY 6

61

LITTLE DAILY STEPS ...OF OBEDIENCE

How do we grow?
Part of the secret
is developing
new ways
to respond to God
and others.
This is the first
of four studies
on new life patterns
that will lead
to joy.

REACT

When
most people hear
the word
"obedience"
they think of . . .

_____

_____

_____

_____

_____

LIST
the words or phrases
each member
of the group
thought of as
"most people's" reaction
to "obedience."

_____   _____

_____   _____

_____   _____

_____   _____

_____   _____

_____   _____

_____   _____

_____   _____

_____   _____

_____   _____

_____   _____

DEFINITION

As you've discovered, many people have different notions about "obedience." But we need to know what definition is used when Scripture speaks to us about obedience to God.

Look over these "is not/is" contrasts. Then on the next page write down your group's definition of obedience. (Be sure to get everyone's input.)

OBEDIENCE

IS NOT a grudging response to duty

IS NOT resentfully doing what is demanded

IS NOT following the path of least resistance

IS NOT always the easy, pleasant pathway

IS NOT a direct path to immediate gain

IS NOT doing what others say is best or right for us.

IS NOT a "legal" kind of thing that keeps us from feeling guilty.

IS personal response to God

IS confidence that God's way is best for you

IS searching out God's will in the Scriptures

IS a conscious commitment of the will to pay the cost of doing right

IS guaranteed by God to lead ultimately to His best

IS letting Christ Himself be Lord in our lives.

IS a love relationship, motivated by and leading to intimacy.

Our definition of obedience to God is:

_____

_____

_____

_____

Now look back
and compare your definition
with "most people's" ideas (p. 65).

MATCH

Here are a list of benefits
of an obedient lifestyle
and verses
which suggest them.
Look up each verse,
and together
match the verse
with the benefit.

BENEFITS OF OBEDIENCE

_____ We find rest and peace in being obedient.
_____ We find greater intimacy in our relationship with God.
_____ We sense God's presence with us.
_____ We find God's direction and guidance for our lives.
_____ We find new confidence in prayer.

BIBLE PASSAGES TO EXPLORE

a. John 14:24

b. 1 John 3:21-22

c. Proverbs 3:5-6

d. Matthew 11:28-29

e. Philippians 4:9

Discuss

If you
have ever experienced
these benefits,
share with the others.

Obedience comes
as "little daily steps"

Obedience flows out of a relationship. God is living within you now, and He speaks to you and me.

Because we are growing persons, we each have much to learn. And God will teach us, though not all at the same speed and not all the same things at the same time.

This is important for us to realize when we speak of "obedience." Because "being obedient" does not mean doing perfectly everything that God describes in the Bible.

Instead the Bible says, "today, if you hear His voice" (Heb. 3:7). Each day God the Spirit will speak to you in the routine of daily living and remind you of what you have learned, and what He wants you to do.

So focus on doing what God is saying to you now. And you will grow more and more obedient as He teaches you daily.

This week

1 Memorize your definition of obedience (p. 67).

2 Share with your partner: Are you a person to whom obedience is easy, or hard? Share too, any truths in this lesson that will help you be responsive to God.

3 Each day read the assigned verse, and think: is it easy or difficult to respond to this kind of God?

JOURNAL

DAY 1   Psalm 115:8

DAY 2   Psalm 145:9

DAY 3   Psalm 145:13

Psalm 145:14   **DAY 4**

Psalm 145:17   **DAY 5**

Psalm 145:18   **DAY 6**

PRACTICING GOD'S WILL 7

Ever wonder how you
could learn and live
by "God's Will?"
Many books have been written
on knowing God's will.
Most have confused
the simplicity of the lifestyle
we see revealed
in the Bible.

GOD'S WILL

GOD'S WORD

**Two sides
of the same
coin**

74

Three discoveries

Let's build a biblical picture of how a person lives "in God's will." We want to find out what actions a person who lives by God's will will take.

We want to find out what the result of a life lived by God's will will be. And we want to see what basic outlook underlies this kind of life.

one

What specific actions *in relationship to the Lord* does the believer need to take to know and experience God's will? *Underline* the key verbs (action words) in the first seven verses of Psalm 37, and write them on the next page.

Do not fret because of evil men
  or be envious of those who do wrong;
for like the grass they will soon wither,
  like green plants they will soon die away.

Trust in the LORD, and do good;
  dwell in the land and enjoy safe pasture.
Delight yourself in the LORD
  and he will give you the desires of your heart.

Commit your way to the LORD
  trust in him and he will do this:
He will make your righteousness shine like the dawn,
  the justice of your cause like the noonday sun.

Be still before the LORD and wait paitently for him;
  do not fret when men succeed in their ways,
  when they carry out their wicked schemes.

Psalm 37:1-7

LIFE
"in God's will"
involves

_____

_____

_____

_____

_____

SHARE

1 Can you illustrate from your own experience what it means to "trust," "delight," "commit your way," "be still," or "wait patiently" for the Lord?

Try to share at least one illustration to help each other better understand these "in the Lord" ways of living.

2 Which of the actions listed is most difficult for you personally? Share with the others and explain why.

two

Look again at Psalm 37:1-7. What does God promise will follow each of these "in-the-Lord" actions? How will your life be affected as you do His will as it is outlined here?

Do not fret because of evil men
   or be envious of those who do wrong;
for like the grass they will soon wither,
   like green plants they will soon die away.

Trust in the LORD and do good;
   dwell in the land and enjoy safe pasture.
Delight yourself in the LORD
   and he will give you the desires of your heart.

Commit your way to the LORD;
   trust in him and he will do this:
He will make your righteousness shine like the dawn,
   the justice of your cause like the noonday sun.

Be still before the LORD and wait patiently for him;
   do not fret when men succeed in their ways,
   when they carry out their wicked schemes.

WRITE
the promised
outcome of life in
God's will

v. 3 _____   v. 5 _____

_____   _____

v. 4 _____   v. 6 _____

_____   _____

PARAPHRASE

Put in your own words, in twentieth-century
terms, what these promises seem to mean
to you.

v. 3 _____   v. 5 _____

_____   _____

v. 4 _____   v. 6 _____

_____   _____

READ
your paraphrases to each other.
If you have questions, ask the other to explain.

three

A Word from Norm

Psalm 37 does not give a formula, but does describe the basic outlook of the child of God. It is in the framework provided by this approach to life that the believer discovers and experiences God's will.

What principles do we see revealed in Psalm 37? Let's look at five.

Rely on God. When Psalm 37 calls on us to "trust in the Lord," the psalmist is making a great statement about Him . . . not about us. Because God is reliable, we are called to look in the Scriptures and discover what God, who speaks only trustworthy words, has said.

Enjoy God. When Psalm 37 invites us to "delight yourself in the Lord," it is again making a statement about God. God is a source of great delight and enjoyment for His people. This gives me confidence that God is for me, and that His will is good. I approach life with this happy orientation.

Commit yourself. On the basis of my understanding of God as a trustworthy and loving person, I now am able to choose freely to obey God. Commitment biblically involves both choosing and following through in action to do what God shows me in the Scriptures.

Don't be anxious. Psalm 37 reminds us that we can "be still" before the Lord. Often we become impatient with circumstances, and our feelings churn. Don't mistake such feelings as the reality. Because God is trustworthy we can be calm and "still" as we wait for Him to act.

Wait patiently. We cannot see our whole life laid out before us, and so cannot really make appropriate "time tables." But God has the full perspective. He is Sovereign, and Trustworthy, and He will bring to pass what is best in our lives.

EXPLORE

We find some things hard to leave in God's hands. Put an
E beside anything you find "easy" to trust God with, and
an H beside any you find "hard."

_____ children's future   _____ on-job relationships

_____ financial needs   _____ personal achievement

_____ health   _____ hostile relationships

_____ national crises   _____ marriage relationships

_____ vocation   _____ others' opinions

_____ non-Christian family members   _____ _____

_____ physical appearance   _____ _____

_____ singleness

Select the one "most difficult" for you.

With your partner, explore the difficult situation.

Then examine the five principles on the preceeding page. Are you
experiencing a breakdown in one or more of these principles in this
area? How might they be applied to resolve the problem?

THIS WEEK

Memorize Matthew
6:33. Telephone
your partner and
pray together for
God's strength in
your "most
difficult" situation.

Journal

DAY 1   Matthew 6:25-26

DAY 2   Matthew 6:27

DAY 3   Matthew 6:28-33

Matthew 6:34   **DAY 4**

Philippians 4:6-7   **DAY 5**

Psalm 32:8-10   **DAY 6**

EXPRESSING YOUR FAITH 8

As a Christian
now
you *are* a new person,
and as you grow
that newness will show.
How will your new life
find expression?

FORM GROUPS OF FOUR

Share with each other
how you became a Christian.
Be sure
to talk about anyone
who was influential
in your decision.
Take about
three minutes each.

INDIVIDUALLY

Fill in this chart about the person(s)
whom you told about
in your group of four.

DESCRIBE WITH KEY WORDS

What was the person like?	
What *actions* influenced you?	
What *words* influenced you?	

TOGETHER

Using your charts from the previous page, combine your observations on this chart to show how we can express our faith in an influential way.

The kind of person who influences

The actions that influence	The words that influence

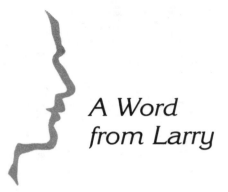

A Word from Larry

What are some of the practical principles* that come from our understanding of witness as overflow?

1 Focus your attention on Jesus. Your effectiveness in witness depends on growing and being filled with Him.

2 Don't wait till you're perfect to say something about the Lord. Your friends will observe the *process of change,* and this is far more compelling evidence of God's presence than the end result!

3 Don't wait till you know everything about the Bible to talk about Jesus. It's life that is at issue, and what you experience is what you have to share. Keep digging in the Bible, certainly. But words of witness are to be focused on Jesus and on your experience with Him.

4 Don't confuse "witness" with talking about your church or trying to get people to go there. It's not wrong to invite people to your church. But you don't want others to "join your religion"; you want them to know Jesus as Savior and find life in Him. So talk about *Him.*

5 You can use a "method" if it seems to help you, but don't rely on it. And don't think that it is the "only way" to point people to Christ. God's basic way to win people to Jesus is to show them Jesus in you, and let you point them to Jesus as you share His "word of reconciliation." Especially, then, don't confuse witnessing with buttonholing strangers. Witnessing focuses on the people you know and who know you.

6 Reach out and get to know nonChristians. If you are a new Christian, you probably have non-Christian friends. Don't cut yourself off from them.

*Richards, *Born to Grow,* pp. 98–99.

WITH
your partner

1 Identify one or two nonChristians you have regular contact with.

2 Look over the principles on page 90 and select one that seems particularly relevant to your relationship with the identified person.

3 Talk and pray together about putting that principle into practice this week.

THIS WEEK

Daily go back over the composite chart on pages 88–89. Ask God to build into your lifestyle the simple and effective ways of expressing your faith in Jesus that you see there.

JOURNAL

_____

DAY 1   1 Peter 2:12

_____

DAY 2   1 Peter 3:15-16

_____

DAY 3   Acts 4:13

1 Timothy 4:12   **DAY 4**

Colossians 3:12   **DAY 5**

Hebrews 13:15-16   **DAY 6**

LIFE TOGETHER

So far
we've talked much
about growing.
Biblically and *practically*
the context for your
continuing growth
is relational.
You will grow
as you continue
to live
your new life
together!

Study

Complete this "together"
Bible study.

Each of the verses
quoted adds more
understanding
of what it means for us
to live in close relationship
with other believers.

Look at the verses
and the INSIGHT
into the key word or phrase.
Then see
if you can share experiences
in which you received
or gave this kind of
loving ministry.

Write in the illustrations.

Accept one another, then, just as
Christ accepted you, in order to
bring praise to God.

Romans 15:7

Stop passing judgment on one
another. Instead make up your
mind not to put any obstacle in
your brother's way.

Romans 14:13

INSIGHT

To "accept" means to welcome;
to invite another in to share your
life.

INSIGHT

To "pass judgment" means to
condemn, look down on, criticize,
things not identified clearly in the
Scriptures as sin.

ILLUSTRATION

ILLUSTRATION

Carry each other's burdens, and in this way you will fulfill the law of Christ. *Galatians 6:2*	Forgive one another, just as in Christ God forgave you. *Ephesians 4:32*	Be kind and compassionate to one another. *Ephesians 4:32*
INSIGHT To "carry burdens" means more than "pray for." It means become involved in practical and personal ways.	INSIGHT Here "forgive" clearly involves a gracious attitude that does not demand repayment for hurts caused by sin's weaknesses.	INSIGHT Kindness and compassion picture a deep sensitivity to others' hurts and needs and a willingness to take initiative in helping.
ILLUSTRATION	ILLUSTRATION	ILLUSTRATION

Let us consider how we may spur one another on to love and good deeds. *Hebrews 10:24*	Let no debt remain outstanding except the debt to love one another. *Romans 13:8*	Now that you have purified yourselves by obeying the truth so that you have sincere love for your brothers, love one another fervently, from the heart. *1 Peter 1:22*
INSIGHT	INSIGHT	INSIGHT
To "spur on" means to motivate, encourage, to stimulate to action. This according to Hebrews is one basic reason for meeting with other Christians.	Love is the one obligation that every Christian has. We "owe it" to each other to love and be loved.	Love is to be an active, conscious, highly motivated involvement in one another's lives.
ILLUSTRATION	ILLUSTRATION	ILLUSTRATION

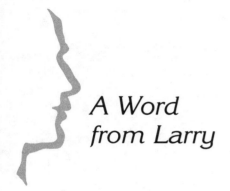

A Word from Larry

When we have the relational climate between members of the Body of Christ described in these "one another" Bible passages, we are in "working order" and ready for growth.

What, then, is "working order" for the body? How does this building up and maturing process happen? Scripture's answer to these questions is clear and simple: you and I are in "working order" when we have the relationship with other believers that God intends. *Personal relationships among Christians are the key to body growth and to the use of our spiritual gifts.*

Love. The critical word in the New Testament about relationships between brothers and sisters in Christ is love. On the night before He was crucified, Jesus gave His disciples careful instructions about the future. Our record of that discussion contains in seed most major teachings of the New Testament. He began His teaching at this point: "A new commandment I give to you, that you love one another, even as I have loved you, that you also love one another. By this all men will know that you are My disciples, if you have love for one another." (John 13:34-35 RSV).

Over and over from this point on, the New Testament stresses love within the body. "Love does no wrong to a neighbor," Romans reminds us; "therefore love is the fulfillment of the law" (Rom. 13:10 RSV). But love is more than not doing wrong. Love is an active, positive reaching out. Love links us together in a bond of unity (Col. 3:14). Love is the goal of the teaching of God's Word (1 Tim. 1:5). We are to "love one another, fervently and from the heart" (1 Peter 1:22, PHILLIPS).*

*Richards, *Born to Grow,* p. 103.

Individually

On the next page are nine circles, one of which represents *you.*

Each of the others represents one of the "one another" relationships you have been studying.

Draw a line between the "you" circle and any other circle(s) which you have *experienced* these last two months. If you *received* this kind of ministry, make an arrow on the line pointing to you. If you *gave* this kind of ministry, make an arrow on the line pointing from you. If you both received and gave, make two arrows.

In the appropriate circle write the name or names of persons with whom these relationships occured.

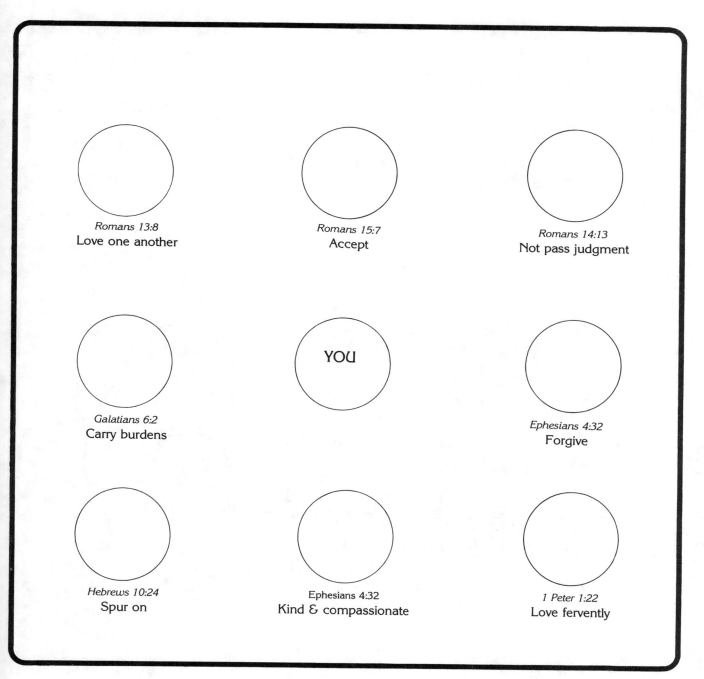

Romans 13:8
Love one another

Romans 15:7
Accept

Romans 14:13
Not pass judgment

Galatians 6:2
Carry burdens

YOU

Ephesians 4:32
Forgive

Hebrews 10:24
Spur on

Ephesians 4:32
Kind & compassionate

1 Peter 1:22
Love fervently

SHARE

If you *received* any of the ministries shown in the circles from members of this study group, take time now to tell them and say "thank you."

THIS WEEK

1 Look back over the "one another" verses. If you are aware of any area in your own life in which one of these ministries would be helpful to you, write on a separate piece of paper a brief description of your need.

2 Sign your name to the above, and include your phone number.

3 Put all your slips of paper in a hat or other container.

4 Now each draw one slip from the container. Rather than meeting with your partner this week, get together with the person whose slip you've drawn.

5 Before you get together, review the need and ask God the way in which you can *best* help meet that need.

JOURNAL

DAY 1   Romans 15:7

DAY 2   Romans 14:13

DAY 3   Romans 13:8

Galatians 6:2   **DAY 4**

Ephesians 4:32   **DAY 5**

Hebrews 10:24   **DAY 6**

GOD OUR FATHER

Moving on
in the Christian life
takes us beyond
new understandings of ourself
and our lifestyle.
Each step we take
brings us
to a new and deeper awareness
of God.

LIKE

Have you ever thought about ways that your earthly
father mirrored (was like) God?

Jot down some traits of your father that you believe
are *like* God's. List them on the "mirror."

UNLIKE

Even the best human being can't reflect God perfectly. Some of us seriously distort God's image.

Jot down on the "mirror" some ways in which you believe your father was *unlike* God.

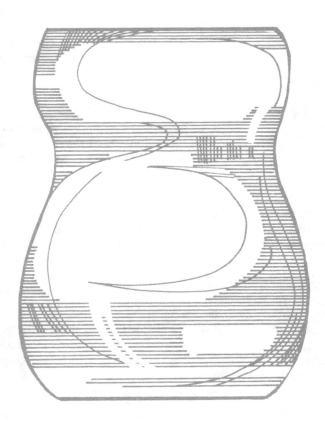

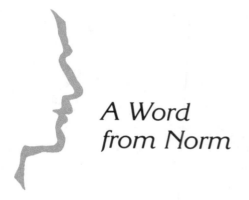

A Word from Norm

Have you ever thought of the significance of the fact that our perception of our Heavenly Father often is shaped by our view of our earthly father?

Sometimes people have difficulty understanding why it is hard for them to relate to God in a comfortable, caring way . . . and have never realized that what they feel about their earthly father is being transferred to their feelings about God! And yet this is just what commonly happens. Our perception of our human father does shape the meaning we give to the word "father," even when we apply that word to "God the Father."

In what ways, for instance, could our experience with our human fathers affect our relationship with God? These may be positive or negative.

ELLA'S father was a stern, judgmental, unaffectionate man. Now in her sixties, Ella wonders why she has never been able to feel close to God. And yet what Ella has been doing is to impose over the Bible's picture of our loving God the impression she retains of fatherhood from her dad.

FRED'S father was undependable. He would make and break promises to the children and to his wife. He consistently put his own interests first, and the family came a distant second. Now Fred wonders about God's trustworthiness, and finds it difficult to commit his problems or himself to the Lord.

TED is a teenager. He has a close relationship with his father and goes to him whenever he wants counsel. His dad will listen, support, and advise him, without dominating or demanding. Ted trusts his father's love and wisdom, and is helped to make good decisions. For Ted personal Bible study, and willingness to be obedient to God, have been made easier by the kind of person his father is.

We can all profit from appreciating in God the traits we've learned to appreciate in our human fathers. And we can all be warned not to let any negative human traits in our fathers distort our understanding of who God really is.

SHARE

in groups of six.

One at a time tell the others the "like" and "unlike" things you wrote on the mirrors on pages 108 and 109.

After each person has shared, the other five should *predict* from the "like" and "unlike" lists those things which may be easy or difficult for the individual in his relationship with God. Use this form for your predictions:

"From the way your father was like God, I think it would be easy for you to . . ."

"From the way your father was not like God, I think it might be difficult for you to . . ."

READ

What is God
the Father like?

The Bible helps us to understand what God the Father is truly like.

We are not left to rely on impressions gained from our parents alone.

In fact, we want to build the meaning of "Father" from our view of God and not our view of our parents.

Look at this story Jesus told and from it develop *as a group* a statement about what God the Father is like. List your insights into the nature of God as Father on the next page.

Jesus continued: "There was a man who had two sons. The younger one said to his father, 'Father, give me my share of the estate.' So he divided his property between them.

"Not long after that, the younger son got together all he had, set off for a distant country and there squandered his wealth in wild living. After he had spent everything, there was a severe famine in that whole country, and he began to be in need. So he went and hired himself out to a citizen of that country, who sent him to his fields to feed pigs. He longed to fill his stomach with the pods that the pigs were eating, but no one gave him anything.

"When he came to his senses, he said, 'How many of my father's hired men have food to spare, and here I am starving to death! I will set out and go back to my father and say to him: Father, I have sinned against heaven and against you. I am no longer worthy to be called your son; make me like one of your hired men.' So he got up and went to his father.

"But while he was still a long way off, his father saw him and was filled with compassion for him; he ran to his son, threw his arms around him and kissed him.

"The son said to him, 'Father, I have sinned against heaven and against you. I am no longer worthy to be called your son.'

"But the father said to his servants, 'Quick! Bring the best robe and put it on him. Put a ring on his finger and sandals on his feet. Bring the fattened calf and kill it. Let's have a feast and celebrate. For this son of mine was dead and is alive again; he was lost and is found.' So they began to celebrate."

Luke 15:11-24

GOD THE FATHER

_____

_____

_____

_____

_____

_____

_____

_____

_____

_____

TOGETHER

How would our lives and attitudes be affected if we saw God clearly as the kind of Father the Bible portrays Him to be—without all the clutter of our own parents' imperfect example?

Build from the view of God as Father you have developed together from the prodigal son story in Luke. Assuming we each know God in this way, make as many "prediction" statements as you can. Use the following format:

"Knowing God as this kind of Father, it will be easy (easier) to . . ."

_____

_____

_____

_____

_____

_____

_____

_____

_____

THIS WEEK

Prayerfully meditate on the following two questions this week.

1 What distortions in my image of God need to be corrected in view of who God really is?

2 What traits revealed in Scripture can I meditate on which will help me know and respond to Him as loving Father?

JOURNAL

DAY 1 1 John 3:1

DAY 2 James 1:16-17

DAY 3 Matthew 6:26

Matthew 7:9-11   **DAY 4**

John 14:21   **DAY 5**

Ephesians 1:3   **DAY 6**

JESUS OUR SAVIOR

One thing
that is exciting to discover
about this "salvation" Jesus brings us
is that it is a
present tense experience,
not only forgiveness
for what is past,
or Heaven promised.
Your steps into deeper faith
are steps
toward a deeper life with Jesus,
our Savior and Lord.

READ
aloud this
story from Larry.

Recently my boys and I went up to the Colorado River near Bullhead City to fish for striped bass. We got our small, 12-foot boat in the water and sped downstream as evening fell, finding fishing the river very different than we expected. Finally, I turned the bow of the boat upstream to return to our car—and was jolted to find that we weren't moving! I had our 7½ horsepower motor wide open, but the current was so swift that we could barely hold our own.

How much this is like the sin within us! Like an awesome current, sin pounds into us, constantly tugging and pulling, clawing at us until it threatens to sweep us along by its power. Too often we are unable to resist its swift downstream flow. All the power within our personalities seems at best able to hold us only briefly against it. And, oh, how easy to slip, and find ourselves carried along and away.

Yet, in presenting Jesus as Savior, the Bible promises you and me the power to move *upstream*. The current will always be there during our earthly life. The tug will always be present within us. But Jesus will be with us too—freeing us from the kind of dilemma my boys and I faced on the river. With Jesus present, the current need not sweep us away, or even hold us back!*

*Richards, *Born to Grow,* pp. 128–29.

LIST

individually three
ways that you feel
sin "tugging" at you
at this point in your
life.

1 _____

_____

2 _____

_____

3 _____

_____

After listing, read on immediately.

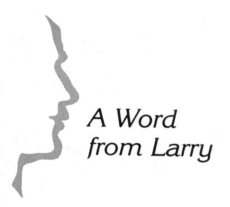

A Word from Larry

A number of truths developed in the Book of Hebrews helps us understand what it means to have Jesus as Savior from *present* sin. But this book, written in New Testament times to Jewish Christians, is hard for some to understand because it uses many Old Testament concepts and pictures.

As background for the verses that you will look at, here are some things you may want to know.

High Priest. The high priest was an individual who represented the whole people of Israel before God. Every year he made a visit to the holiest place in the temple, with a blood offering for past sins. Then he was forced to leave that place of God's special presence.

The New Testament identifies Jesus as our High Priest. What is different about Him? First, he *always lives* to represent us. No death or weakness can keep Jesus from speaking up for *you* in God's presence. There is another difference. The High Priest in Old Testament times only came once a year, and briefly, into God's most intimate holy place. But Jesus, because of His sacrifice of Himself on Calvary, entered heaven itself. He is now there, in the very presence of the Father.

From the throne of the greatest power in the universe Jesus, as our representative with God, offers us power to help against the tug of sin and assures us of the mercy of continuing forgiveness if we should ever give in.

DISCUSS TOGETHER

Which of these reactions are most likely to be yours when you feel the tug of sin? Share, and add other reactions if necessary.

guilt

defensiveness

hopelessness (defeatism)

anger

shame

fear

self-condemnation

isolation from God

other _____

Why do you think you react as you do?

READ

these passages from the Book of Hebrews. Draw information from them to complete the chart on the next page.

Therefore, since we have a great high priest who has gone through the heavens, Jesus the Son of God, let us hold firmly to the faith we profess. For we do not have a high priest who is unable to sympathize with our weaknesses, but we have one who has been tempted in every way, just as we are—yet was without sin. Let us then approach the throne of grace with confidence, so that we may receive mercy and find grace to help us in our time of need.

Hebrews 4:14–16

Now there were many of those priests, since death prevented them from continuing in office; but because Jesus lives forever, he has a permanent priesthood. Therefore he is able to save completely those who come to God through him, because he always lives to intercede for them.

Such a high priest meets our need—one who is holy, blameless, pure, set apart from sinners, exalted above the heavens. Unlike the other high priests, he does not need to offer sacrifices day after day, first for his own sins, and then for the sins of the people. He sacrificed for their sins once for all when he offered himself. For the law appoints as high priests men who are weak; but the oath, which came after the law, appointed the Son, who has been made perfect forever.

Hebrews 7:23–28

Therefore, brothers, since we have confidence to enter the Most Holy Place by the blood of Jesus, by a new and living way opened for us through the curtain, that is, his body, and since we have a great priest over the house of God, let us draw near to God with a sincere heart in full assurance of faith, having our hearts sprinkled to cleanse us from a guilty conscience and having our bodies washed with pure water. Let us hold unswervingly to the hope we profess, for he who promised is faithful. And let us consider how we may spur one another on toward love and good deeds. Let us not give up meeting together, as some are in the habit of doing, but let us encourage one another—and all the more as you see the Day approaching.

Hebrews 10:19-25

JESUS' PAST ACTIONS	JESUS' PRESENT MINISTRIES	WE ARE NOW FREED TO . . .

READ

Jennie, like the rest of us, experiences that inner tug of sin. In many areas she's able to simply make a decision . . . and stand by it. She's been learning to take those little steps of "obedience" we looked at earlier.

Sometimes though—and with some special problems—it's not that easy. Jennie makes the decision all right: "I won't!" But then, at times just a few minutes afterward, the whole thing just seems to fall apart and she's doing what she determined she would not.

There are times when temptation in those problem areas comes that Jennie gets very frustrated: almost despondent, or fearful. She's sure that no matter what she says she'll do, when the time to act comes she'll make the wrong choice. Both guilt and shame come in then, and Jennie even questions her relationship with God at times.

It's also particularly hard later, looking back on her failure. She has a hard time excusing herself for her actions. And she wonders how God must feel about her failure. At times like these it's very hard to read the Bible or pray or even think about the Lord. She just wants to sort of keep away . . . and pull into herself and hide.

Jennie is experiencing the pain of sin present: the pain that is caused by the principle of sin at work in a human being's life day to day. Jennie needs to learn more of what it means to have Jesus as Savior in her present, as well as in her past and for her eternal future.

DISCUSS

1 There's a process that takes place from the first tug of a temptation, through struggle with it, to either victory or defeat. Try to
   define the *critical times* in a process like the one Jennie is
   experiencing.

2 When you have agreed on the critical times in the process of our
   present tense struggle with sin, look back on the chart on page
   125. How does Jesus as Savior relate to each problem area?

3 Imagine yourselves counselors to a person like Jennie. In view of
   what the Bible says about Jesus' present work as Savior, how
   would you advise Jennie if she came to you for guidance?
   Imagine that she comes, at different times, at each of the critical
   times you've defined. Work out principles of how to respond for
   each time and list these principles on the next page in the space
   provided.

LIST

helpful principles
to apply
when you deal with
the tug of sin
in your own life,
remembering this
is possible
because Jesus *is*
Savior now.

_____

_____

_____

_____

_____

_____

_____

CONCLUDE

Share with your partner the three areas you listed
on page 121 where you feel sin's tug in your life.
Talk over anything in this session that has been
helpful and pray together.

THIS WEEK

Review the
principles you listed
on the previous
page. Try to
become sensitive to
opportunities to
apply them.

JOURNAL

Matthew 11:28-30   **DAY 1**

John 6:27-29, 35   **DAY 2**

John 10:1-18   **DAY 3**

DAY 4 John 14:15-27

DAY 5 John 15:1-17

DAY 6 John 17:1-14

THE HOLY SPIRIT

The third person
of the Trinity
is someone
less known than
the Father and Son.
What we discover
in Scripture
is exciting:
He is God's gift
to us.
He is our constant
companion!

A Word from Larry

Read this brief article and circle key words that help you understand the Holy Spirit and His ministry.

God's gift. This is the first exciting thing about the Holy Spirit. He is the Father's gift to us. Jesus told His disciples on the crucifixion eve, "I tell you the truth, it is to your advantage that I go away; for if I do not go away, the Helper shall not come to you; but if I go, I will send Him to you" (John 16:7). It was better for them (and for us) that God the Holy Spirit come than that the Son stay!

The Spirit's name here is important: *Helper.* Sometimes translated *Comforter,* the term means in the original to *stand alongside.* Jesus' leaving didn't mean that His followers were to be deserted. Far from it. After Jesus' resurrection and ascension, God the Holy Spirit was sent as our permanent companion. In the Person of the Holy Spirit,

God takes His stand with us. He is *here.* In every situation, the Helper we need to give us strength and wisdom is with us!

This is the first thing to know. God the Holy Spirit is your constant companion, standing with you, eager to provide the help you need.

Yours, now. Sometimes we find it hard to grasp. God has given Himself to us. Doubting, we revert to our old ways and attitudes and begin to feel that we have to do something to merit such a gift. Certainly we ought at least to *tarry*—to beg God for the gift and wait steadfastly for it. At least, this is what some feel.

But remember our earlier chapters? Remember that God says, "How shall He not with Him [Jesus], also freely give us all things?" (Rom. 8:32 KJV). God's way of relating to us is in grace. God intends to give freely. This is just what He has done in giving us the Spirit!

Romans 8:9 puts it clearly. "If anyone does not have the Spirit of Christ, he does not belong to Him." And, yet more positively, 1 Corinthians 12 shows that each believer not only has the Holy Spirit with Him, he also has a Spirit-given gift! Upon our conversion, the Holy Spirit came to us, and He Himself became the link that joins us to Jesus and each other (1 Cor. 12:13). You don't have to *ask* for the Spirit, or beg. The Holy Spirit is with you now, and He'll stay with you as a divine pledge that you will always be God's child: a divine Presence to let you know that you are a most precious possession of your heavenly Father (Eph. 1:13-14).*

*Richards, *Born to Grow,* pp. 137–38.

SHARE

Together, each share one insight about the
Holy Spirit which is particularly meaningful
to you.

The Holy Spirit is with us to give us productive and meaningful lives.

But what does the Holy Spirit produce in our lives? And how will that product make your life more meaningful? Study the following passages and complete the charts individually.

The fruit of the Spirit is love, joy, peace, patience, kindness, goodness, faithfulness, gentleness, and self-control.

Galatians 5:22-23

But the Counselor, the Holy Spirit, whom the Father will send in my name, will teach you all things and will remind you of everything I have said to you.

John 14:26

THE SPIRIT PRODUCES

THE SPIRIT PRODUCES

IMPORTANT TO ME BECAUSE

IMPORTANT TO ME BECAUSE

When he [the Spirit] comes, he will convict the world of sin in regard to guilt and righteousness and judgment.

John 16:8

And if the Spirit of him who raised Jesus from the dead is living in you, he who raised Christ from the dead will also give life to your mortal bodies through his Spirit, who lives in you.

Romans 8:11

THE SPIRIT PRODUCES

THE SPIRIT PRODUCES

IMPORTANT TO ME BECAUSE

IMPORTANT TO ME BECAUSE

In the same way, the Spirit helps us in our weakness. We do not know what we ought to pray, but the Spirit himself intercedes for us with groans that words cannot express.

Romans 8:26

Now to him who is able to do immeasurably more than all we ask or imagine, according to the power that is at work within us, to him be glory in the church and in Christ Jesus throughout all generations, forever and ever, Amen.

Ephesians 3:20–21

THE SPIRIT PRODUCES

THE SPIRIT PRODUCES

IMPORTANT TO ME BECAUSE

IMPORTANT TO ME BECAUSE

CHECK

Go back over the last few pages and place a check by the things the Spirit has already produced in your life.

SHARE

In groups of six share your insights into why His presence is important to you.

RANK

The Bible teaches that God the Spirit is with us to help us in many significant ways. Here is a list of six ministries of the Spirit to us. Rank the top *two* by importance to you where you are now.

_____ The Spirit is with me to comfort me in times of loneliness.

_____ The Spirit is with me to encourage me when I find it hard to make important decisions.

_____ The Spirit is with me to help me understand the Scripture.

_____ The Spirit is with me to help me pray.

_____ The Spirit is with me to help my character develop the fruit of love, patience, etc.

_____ The Spirit is with me to convince others of their need for God when I speak about Jesus with them.

FORM

a group with others
who ranked the same ministry
that you did
as of number one priority.

SHARE

why you chose this item.
Then pray together,
thanking God for His gift
of the Spirit,
and for each other,
that you might experience
this ministry of the Spirit
this week.

THIS WEEK

From the daily Bible readings in your journal choose *one* word that
describes the kind of relationship God wants you to experience with
the Holy Spirit. Visualize this experience happening in your life.

JOURNAL

Galatians 5:22-23   **DAY 1**

John 14:26   **DAY 2**

John 16:8-11   **DAY 3**

141

DAY 4   Romans 8:11

DAY 5   Romans 8:26

DAY 6   Ephesians 3:20-21

LOOKING AHEAD 13

The Christian life
is a life
of continual growth:
personally,
in relationship with each other,
and in relationship
with God.
Now is a good time
to pause to look back—
and ahead.

SHARE

Form a large circl...
and place a chair i...
One by one
take the center ch...
one of the followin...

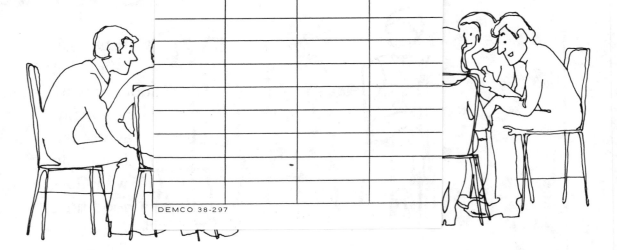

DATE DUE

DEMCO 38-297

1 What have I discovered about God that has been meaningful to me?

2 How have my relationships with others in the group been helpful to me?

3 What have I discovered about myself that gives me hope and confidence for the future?